Mental Illness

Acceptance, Prevention, Cure, Psychopathy and Beyond

AMARPREET SINGH

THE THOUGHT FLAME
TURNING SPARK INTO FLAME

info@thethoughtflame.com

www.thethoughtflame.com

Table of Contents

Introduction 1

Chapter One: What Is Mental Illness? 4

Chapter Two: Rare Types of Mental

Disorders 14

Chapter Three: Is Mental Illness

Preventable? 21

Chapter Four: Risk Factors of Developing

Mental Illness...31

Chapter Five: The Difference Between

Psychopathy and Mental Illness 37

Chapter Six: Different Signs and Symptoms

of Mental Illness... 47

Chapter Seven: How To Best Deal With

Mental Illness.. 52

Chapter Eight: Real Life Solutions To

Conquer Your Mental Illness In Your

Personal Life and In Society 69

Conclusion 78
About Us 81
Author 83

Introduction

Out of all the true things about life, the most brutal yet the most honest one is that it's full of sufferings. You may sleep in a bed of roses tonight but tomorrow you'll be made to walk a path of thorns. It is no secret that whoever dreamt of life as a wish granting factory has always witnessed evidences to its contrary.

This book has been written with an objective of walking you through the different causes, symptoms, treatments and precautionary measures associated with one of the trickiest part of the human body and mind.

He who harms the body creates physical damage; he who harms the mind creates much more. Our mind is not an assembly line, which has been programmed to churn out solutions against dire circumstances and desperate times. At times, it needs its naps and requires some rejuvenation of its own. When it is deprived of the same and laden with more burdens, it suffers irreparable fractures. Now, these fractures may either slow you down temporarily or cause you long lasting suffering. While the former is easy to deal with, the latter requires some graver steps than mere coping up.

There's only one person in the whole wide world who could help you gather yourself up and stand up back from mental stress; it's you. A lot in the book will be centered on how you deal with the issue and not how you get help from others. The rest of it will talk about what all steps you can take to ensure recovery by engaging external inputs.

In this book you will learn how to spot sure symptoms of mental and illness and what could possibly cause the condition in the first place. Above all you will learn how to best cope with these symptoms so you can overcome what kind of trouble may head your way.

Chapter One: What Is Mental Illness?

A mental illness can be defined as a behavioral pattern, which impairs your mind and makes the body act abnormally in social circles. It is a set of many disorders that put obstacles in the path of your mental behavior's normal functioning. It leads you to think, act, perceive and interpret differently than how you would have done if you were not affected by it. Mental illness is a general name given to all the problems faced by your mind while trying to function generally.

The statistics (NAMI.org) reveal that 60 million Americans suffer with some form of mental illness every year. That breaks down to one in four people. New studies reveal an alarming statistic of one out of every two Americans falling victim to some form of mental illness at some point in their lives.

When the brain misfires, when someone does not see or experience the world the way most people do, the consequences run deep and far-reaching. In fact, mental illness, as the number one health care expense, drains families, communities and the government to the tune of $ 100 billion dollars annually.

When people cannot take proper care of themselves they wind up relying on others to supply housing, medical treatments, food – all the necessities of survival. The homeless on the street sleeping in boxes - they lack the mental faculties to get a job, to get help and to contribute to society.

Those people, who society labels as derelicts, wind up in court, in jail or prison, and occasionally in special education programs instead of in training programs to help them build a more independent life. The slightly higher functioning mentally ill live in privately supported and government facilities where tax monies fund their huge expenses of living.

Is this really living though?

For many people diagnosed with chronic mental illness they see a world to which they do not really belong. Some of them, aware of their differences, plunge into depression and hopeless. They suffer the pain of knowing their lives do not look like they want them to. You can witness that despair in the art created by many patients with diagnoses including schizophrenia and depression, bipolar and anxiety.

Knowing they have problems, even recognizing why they suffer, never eliminates the pain. Unfortunately, releasing their frustration and hurt in very visible and tangible forms fails to lead them out of the darkness that envelops them. Indeed, focusing on their pain and what is missing from their lives serves to increase the suffering. They have no idea how to break free from their prisons.

The psychiatric care industry, formed to help them, often reflects misguided ways to medicate , to keep them medicated and in therapy that may or may not help change their dilemma at all. Basically, many programs and treatments are about managing their lives, keeping them safe – from themselves and others – and keeping others safe from them. On top of all that stress add reactions from a society that stigmatizes their predicament, a society who is, bottom line, afraid of them.

Ignorance keeps them from getting to know, to hire or socialize with, to honor and respect people with labels like schizophrenia, bipolar, depression, anxiety, borderline and attention deficit and hyperactivity – among others.

Healthy people want to feel safe. They want the mentally deviants kept out of sight – their sight – so they themselves are out of harm's way physically, emotionally and spiritually. People fear what they do not know.

Do not misunderstand, many professionals assume what they do works and must be safe. Even the doctors prescribing those drugs often believe them to be safe and effective. The truth gets buried as it does in all other fields that prey upon public ignorance.

The Different Types of Mental Illness

1. Personality Disorder

If a medical expert were asked to pick the gravest category of mental disorder, chances are pretty high that he'd name this one. The difference between this and the other sub categories is that this is of the severest degree possible. The rest of the disorders do not play with your personality; this one does. The person is so messed up from inside that their normal environments like home, school, college and work start getting affected.

2. Post Traumatic Stress Disorder or PTSD

Like it was mentioned at the start of this book, life is full of let downs. Rainbows and cupcakes exist in fairy tales and Disney movies. Humans are bound to face failures one day or another. Some failures have so great an impact on our minds that their effect is not only traumatic but also long lasting. We are not able to get over the scars for a long time; at times forever. The distresses caused because of an unfortunate event, like for example the passing away of a parent or a heat break are covered under this sub category.

3. Varying Types of Anxiety Disorder

Those afflicted with anxiety disorders tend to respond to certain things, circumstances, words or actions as if they were a threat or an absurdity. Dread is the most common lens used to look through by such people. Anxiety disorder can manifest itself in the form of physical reactions as well, like a rapid heartbeat or profuse and immediate sweat spots appearing on your forehead. All the kinds of phobias that you have heard of including the fear of enclosed spaces, of heights, of water, of pets, they are all included under this.

4. Psychotic Disorders

A person is said to have been suffering from psychotic disorder if he's been imagining things or been having disassociated thoughts and performing actions that do not match their intentions.

Psychotic disorders affect that part of the brain, which is responsible for imagination. They not only switch on the imagination tap but also help it leak to its maximum; so much so that people do not remain competitive enough to tell the difference between what is real and what is not. Schizophrenia is a good example for this kind of mental illness

5. Mood Disorders

Ever felt sudden happiness and the next moment extreme sadness? If the answer is yes, then you are probably suffering from a mood disorder. A mood disorder is a medical term given to what we commonly call 'mood swings'. It is the swaying of your mood from being over enthusiastically joyous to pitch dark distress. There is no in between. The middle picture is missing and whenever you are with such people you can clearly tell, which extreme they are going through right now.

6. Addiction Disorders

Although addiction disorders should involve substance abuse and drug overdose issues but the condition is more than just about usage of drugs. The urge to overdose on drugs is an addiction disorder. Two most commonly abused things are drugs and alcohol. Those affected by addiction disorders are so attached to the mentioned substances that they start establishing relationships with them and refuse to let go of the want to consume them.

7. Obsessive Compulsive Disorder or OCD

Some humans cannot let go of some of their dearest held and religiously followed routines and rituals. Such rituals may seem trivial to others but to them it is the only way to do a certain act. If deviated, they feel distressed and miserable. In order to make sure that a particular routine is strictly followed, they are willing to go to any lengths, most of the time at the cost of time, money, social acceptance and physical energy.

Chapter Two: Rare Types of Mental Disorders

Some mental illnesses are rare, but the severity of such conditions is extreme, making them infamous in the medical world. There are also psychotic disorders that don't just affect a person's behavior, but also the brain and its cognitive thinking. This type of mental illness interferes with "reality" in the eyes of the person, making him or her unable to live normally in any way. For example, schizophrenia is a condition in which a person has more than one personality and an inability to tell reality apart from fantasy.

Another known but rare condition is the infamous Manic Bipolar Disorder. People with schizophrenia develop delusional beliefs that start out as simple fantasies that later take over their lives almost completely. Sometimes, these delusions are involuntary. In addition, schizophrenics have a complicated set of behaviors and ways of thinking. Not only are schizophrenics paranoid, they may also be depressive and anxious, but in such extreme levels that they can neither think clearly, nor face choices or changes.

Schizophrenia

The main characteristics of schizophrenia are disorganized thinking, severe paranoia and/ or anxiety, and a disconnection from reality. People with this condition experience hallucinations: hearing voices or seeing apparitions that are not really there. When told that these experiences are unreal, a schizophrenic might deny the truth to the extent of becoming aggressive. Schizophrenic individuals also experience phantom pains. The unreal experiences affect their way of thinking, disrupting it and leading them to disbelieve others, even loved ones.

Confusion is inevitable in this condition, and cognitive thinking is greatly affected. This kind of mental illness not only affects the afflicted person, but also the people around him or her. They are not mentally capable of doing certain jobs. It is unsafe for them to be left alone, and it is also unsafe for them to be in crowded places. People who are diagnosed with schizophrenia are considered self- destructive, and they may also pose a possible threat to others. The schizophrenic individual is not just emotionally unstable, but has no strength to control their illness, making them unpredictable and sometimes prone to inhumane actions.

Types of Schizophrenics

1. **The Disorganized Type**-this type of schizophrenia is characterized by general

disorganization. People with this type of disorder suddenly talk gibberish or recite songs, poems, or scripts, and they do so for no apparent reason. They might even invent a language of their own or simply speak out meaningless words. Some will suddenly laugh, sob, or giggle by themselves , obviously caught up and lost in their own thoughts.

2. The Paranoid Type-paranoid type schizophrenics have extreme anxiety and fear. Their paranoia revolves around the suspicion that someone, a surreal being or secret organization, is out to capture or hurt them. A paranoid schizophrenic may also feel that others are harassing him or are scheming to overthrow, murder, or harm him in some way. People who are paranoid schizophrenic have a tendency to argue excessively with others, act aloof, and display fits of anger or rage. They have the unusual belief that there is either a known or unknown enemy nearby.

3. The Undifferentiated Type-this type has some of the characteristics of the other types of schizophrenia. The individual may have paranoid symptoms as well as disorganization. What makes this type of schizophrenic separate is that the symptoms are not equally evident and are only transitional, if not temporary, and no symptoms are intense enough to categorize the person under a single type.

4. The Residual Type-this simply means "leftovers" of a previous or past history of schizophrenia in a person. There are some symptoms of the condition left that may indicate a major outburst followed by complete remission, or simply no more occurrences for the rest of the individual's life.

Manic Bipolar Disorder

This disorder is infamous for its extremely noticeable characteristics. Like schizophrenics, manic-bipolar individuals have a false sense of reality and tend to live in their own thoughts of fantasy. People with this condition believe they are an entirely different person; for example, the Queen of Sheba, an ex-convict hiding from government forces, or an alien envoy from another galaxy. Their perception of reality is so altered that they have no sense of time, place, or what is happening to them. Manic bipolar individuals will suddenly act a certain way without warning, possibly hurting others. Some individuals with bipolar disorder simply stop moving or speaking for hours.

Infamous cases involve individuals talking nonsensical things, putting make-up on, and dressing in unusual ways. Some of the most serious cases involve the individual stopping in the middle of his or her activities, including walking. The person maintains this "pose" for hours without disturbance. Others may try to provoke the individual to move or speak, but to no avail. The danger in this is that the return of motion is unpredictable; it may take days before the manic bipolar resumes his activities, and sometimes when he does, he is aggressive.

Schizophrenia and manic bipolar disorder are chronic mental illnesses that require multiple medications alongside psychotherapy and moral support. Some cases take years to treat , and most individuals with these disorders experience recurring symptoms with remissions before finally achieving more stable mental health. Remissions are lingering episodes or periods of time when the afflicted individual experiences a mentally healthy state. The symptoms of their illness are absent for a time being, but the cycle ends at some point , and the onset of the symptoms returns. Not all mental illnesses have remissions; some are consistent, while other symptoms grow less in severity but are still present.

Chapter Three: Is Mental Illness Preventable?

Let's talk about new paradigms – that really are not new – in the field of mental illness. IT is not brain chemistry going out of whack that creates symptoms. IT is hormonal imbalances , inflammation, toxins and parasites crossing the blood brain barrier that should be there that cause psychological malfunction. Add to that list of malnutrition, skull bone misalignment, spinal misalignment, dehydration and inadequate rest.

What does this mean?

Well, a pioneer in the field of orthomolecular psychiatry, Dr. Carl Pfieffer formulated, through expensive research on children and adults, Pfeiffer's Law that stated, "For every drug that benefits a patient, there is a natural substance that can achieve the same effect." It is important to not that during a crisis, like a psychotic episode – drugs may be needed to prevent harm to the aggressor or toward others. I am talking sedative and for the moment not as routine for life. Drugs do have their place. However, nutrition should always be the first choice – once the crisis passes. Drugs must be the last resort.

Back in the 1970s, at the Brain Bio Center at Princeton University, Dr. Pfeiffer's team reversed schizophrenia and learning disabilities - including ADD, ADHD, and dyslexia in children - using zinc and vitamin B6. His work expanded to the known characteristics of other mental illness diagnoses – categorizing them and determining the nutritional supplements needed to produce healthy bodies and eliminate brain misfiring.

So, what is the potential cause of most of these debilitating illnesses?

Diet is the root cause of very many physical and mental issues. Make that diet and water. The fact is that serial killers, schizophrenics, people who act out – show mineral deficiencies in the brain.

It takes years to develop those deficiencies. A child born with normal healthy flora damages that natural healthy state by eating poorly. The health decline begins almost immediately when the child is bottle fed rather than breast-fed. Human flora is intended to nourish people. Animal milk hosts flora intended for animals not for humans. Right from the start that child is fighting to digest what it consumes.

consumes. The problem intensifies when the mother, whose poor eating habits and unhealthy gut, passed on her digestive system maladies to the child. If mom had a compromised system from eating fast food and processed foods, chemical and microwaved food, then the child's well being is at risk.

That's why psychotic breaks – as seen in schizophrenia and bipolar disorder – usually begin between the ages of eighteen and twenty-five. They result from the massive deficiencies of minerals and vitamins in the brain created over a lifetime.

All during childhood, digestive issues prevailed and multiple learning disabilities crept in. Those are the signs to look for in a child – the signs that preceded mental health issues. Other common health problems include being a picky eater, a colicky baby, constipation, impaction, ear, nose and throat infections and consumption of antibiotics.

Full-blown mental illness usually does not show until later in life though it the groundwork is happening in the gut from an early age.

Educate yourself about nutrition . Your life depends on it. The life of the child entrusted in your care depends on eating well , on eating food that is nutritious, on eating organic non-chemical , non-toxic food, and on eating real - not processed, not sugared, not artificially flavored or sweetened, and definitely not microwaved food.

The human body was designed to eat high quality organic , pure, humanely treated clean animal proteins and animal fat and to eat it cooked – but not overcooked. Yes, cooking may destroy some nutrition in the food. However, raw food with high fiber is not digestible by many people. The whole point of fiber is that it is not digested and theoretically will clean out the gut.

Water is another essential for the brain wellness. But not just any water. You need to drink water that your body actually uses to gain and maintain health. You want to drink water that is alkaline and oxygenated, has a hexagonal structure and is broken down into easily assimilated small molecule clumps by magnets. You want your water to have natural minerals in it or you will not be able to use it.

In the end, I have found that the cause of many mental illnesses today comes down to nutrition and hydration. Do both and you should be able to prevent mental illness in as early as fetal development.

Of course we have to accept the fact that all of us are damaged in some way or another. It takes a great deal of bravery to admit that we are; a greater deal more to do something about it. Most of the times people ignore signs that undoubtedly point towards the sign that says '' something's wrong with you''. The first step therefore, is noticing and acknowledging. It's a long yet doable path to recovery after this stage.

The truth of the matter is that mental illnesses are not very rare in this century. With the corporate wheels grinding and the clocks ticking down our necks all the time, burden, distress, rage and anxiety have become acquirable. The rat race that life has become rarely lets us find time for our mind's relaxation. Without getting the time to catch its breath, our minds keep working shifts after shifts and get worn out in the end. It is during such times that all sorts of mental disorders start invading.

Common Causes of Mental Illness

1. Physical Violence

Not everyone's childhood is about fairs and joyrides. We all have traumatic childhood experiences that shudder down the spine whenever we are reminded of it. A past event, which involved physical aggression can very well cause a mental fracture and bring in an effect that can be categorized as a mental illness.

2. Past and Current Failures

We all fail. For without failing, the taste of success just isn't that sweet. But some of us take the fall so hard that not only do we forget to get up but we also tend to harbor a phobia of ever getting up again. Real life failures at times push us so deep down in to the pits that to be able to gather our strength for a recovery becomes difficult.

3. Possible Medical Causes

The brain is the most powerful and the most sensitive organ of the human body. While it has the potential to think up the greatest of invention, it's also got the capacity to shut an individual down. Imagine it to be a Rolls Royce car. It can help you get the attention on the road but if left unattended and ignored, or say if there's a nut missing in one of its important machine parts, it is futile to continue owning it. At times, our brain plays with us.

This behavior of the brain could result out of two things: Accidents or Hormones. Under this category, genetics are also covered. Some mental disorders get passed down the generations and you are simply unlucky to have been born with those genes.

4. A Variety of Other Reasons

Other than the mentioned causes, there are arrays of reasons why people suffer from mental illnesses. Sexual advances when not consented to or overly done may cause a person to undergo great trauma. Some people are not meant to be social. They do not feel the need to come in contact with the society.

Such cases are wrongly named as anti socials; the proper term is unsocial. They are at a high risk of getting visited by various mental disorders. Those who have been victims of crimes are also prone to get attacked by mental disorders.

It matters not whether they got justice or not. The very experience of having gone through the crime is reason enough for them to get into depression. Unless treated with care and extreme caution, such people tend to travel deeper into the problem with a promise to never recover despite all the assistance being offered to them.

Chapter Four: Risk Factors of Developing Mental Illness

If you are wondering whether or not you may have developed a mental illness, there are certain risks that could make that possible. In this chapter we will explore the different risk factors associated with Mental Illness so you can get a better understanding of whether or not you may be able to develop a mental illness later on in life.

Mental Illness Is An Increased Risk For Alcoholics

Have you got a psychological illness in your family, or are there any family members of yours who are battling with depression and alcoholism? Did you know that if one of your family members suffers with any one of these disorders, that your chances of suffering from one are also increased? Once you have discovered which mental disorder you might have, it is time to get help as quickly as possible. If you are a teenager and you live with a parent who drinks, you may not be aware of what alcohol can do to your body.

Research indicates that the younger the brain, the more it may be at risk, and because as a young person, your brain will still be developing, and if you drink excessively, you may actually be destroying some of your mental capacity, and also affecting your ability to learn. You are susceptible to damage in two parts of the brain which are still developing; the pre-frontal cortex which is important for decision making, and the hippocampus, a part of the brain responsible or learning and memory.

Uncertainty

If you are living in an uncertain environment where you are uncertain about your future , your progress and your whole life then it would subject you to develop mental illnesses more quickly as compared to anyone who stays in a well balanced society with assurance of a bright future ahead.

Lack of Tolerance

Lack of tolerance acts double ways to damage your personality. Not only it will keep you at high risk of developing biological as well as psychological malfunctions but it will also make the life situations worst.

How To Test Yourself For A Mental Illness

How do you know which mental disorder you have? There are so many mental disorders in the world today and medical experts have put quizzes or questionnaires on the Internet which can give you an indication as to which particular medical disorder you have or are prone to.

These tests aren't diagnostic tools, but rather a tool to provide some insight into a potential disorder you may have. Some of the questions asked in these tests include asking for your age, gender, whether you take actions without thinking about the consequences, whether your moods fluctuate a lot, whether you find it hard to concentrate on something for a long time, and whether you are plagued by suspicions that other people may be planning and doing things behind your back. You can answer these questions and submit the questionnaire and get the answer that will serve as a guide to taking action immediately before the mental disorder gets out of hand.

Simply Look and Listen

If you believe that you have any one of the many disorders there are, you will want to know how to recognize the words and behavior patterns that go hand in hand with such an illness. Sometimes before resorting to the help of a medical professional, you will be glad to know that there are self-help strategies that can first be attempted to boost your emotional health. You want to be a person who is emotionally healthy and who is able to handle life's challenges.

You will also no doubt want to be the kind of person who is in control of their emotions and who is able to bounce back and recover from life's setbacks. Everyone wants to have a sense of contentment about them, the ability to deal with stress and the ability to learn new things and adapt to change, and for this reason you want to know how to look out for symptoms in yourself that might indicate a mental disorder.

Being in a good state of mental health isn't about the absence of mental health problems; it is being emotionally healthy so that you are able to deal with the health problems as they come your way. Before you visit a medical expert, there are some things you can do to help yourself handle stress in a better way. You will want to find things in your life that make you feel positive and emotionally healthy.

Chapter Five: The Difference Between Psychopathy and Mental Illness

The term psychopathy was coined in 1941 by a psychiatrist named Hervey M. Cleckley to describe specific traits and behavioral patterns. In a nutshell, psychopaths are said to be charming and seemingly normal at first— but they have an underlying callousness and egoism that make them capable of doing hurtful things simply for the sake of fun and enjoyment. All they care about is their personal well-being, and they don't mind lying or doing whatever it takes to get what they want.

Psychopaths are highly rational, but they are known to be undependable and irresponsible because they don't exhibit regular human emotions like empathy, guilt, or even love.

They are very impulsive, and when things go wrong in their plans, they'll find someone else to take the blame for them. They don't listen to the words of other people and will continue head-on with their own plans.

Psychopaths are easily lured into criminal activity when they think they will be able to get away with it. Calculating, devious, and controlling, psychopaths are very dangerous when crossed. Psychopaths make up roughly 1% of the global population, and studies suggest that the majority of them are male.

It is true that many criminals can be considered psychopaths— one study suggests that an estimated 25%, or 1 out of 4 criminals in jail meet the diagnostic criteria for psychopathy. But these criminals are surely not the only psychopaths that walk the earth, are they?

In fact, most psychopaths are not criminals — and one might even be close to you. If not for their tendency to develop erratic and impulsive behaviors, a lot of psychopaths would be successful in their careers.

That being said, psychopaths tend to find high-flying and glamorous jobs more appealing than regular ones since having an impressive job strokes their egos. Corporate CEO-ship, lawmaking and enforcement, politics, clergy, and media practice are all potentially attractive job prospects for a psychopath.

The Traits Of A Psychopath

Psychiatrists and psychologists alike have come up with several diagnostic instruments to gauge psychopathy. Cleckley himself has devised a list of traits often displayed by psychopaths . A Canadian psychologist, Robert Hare, also created the Psychopathy Checklist-Revised (PCL-R), a popular 20-question checklist used to diagnose the incidence of psychopathy.

There is a general consensus among these diagnostic instruments about the common traits of a psychopath. The list includes the following traits, tendencies, and behavioral patterns.

Charming and Intelligent

Psychopaths are smooth talkers, and they easily turn on a superficial kind of charm that leaves a false good impression on the people they meet. They are very verbose, and you'd never find one who gets tongue-tied or shy around other people.

Narcissism

In a psychopath's way of thinking, the world revolves around them. Everything has to be about them: their needs, their wants, their desires. Anything else beyond that doesn't exist for them.

Constant Lying

At the very least, a psychopath may simply be cunning, shrewd , or clever. At the most, psychopaths have a tendency to carry out full-blown deceptions and manipulating others for their own interests. They can be underhanded, and because of their shallowness, they are without scruples in their deception tactics.

Easily Bored

Psychopaths are thrill-seekers. They thrive on excitement and danger. They love taking risks and tend to get bored with routine. This is why most psychopaths find it difficult to hold on to jobs and end up drifting on the fringes of society.

Manipulation

Once they're sure that they can get away with it, psychopaths tend to use their deception techniques to control other people for personal gain . Cheating and fraudulent activities may be typical fare for a manipulative psychopath.

No Remorse

Psychopaths don't feel any twinges of conscience for what they have done, because they have no value judgment abilities, and a warped sense of right and wrong. The only emotion they may display towards other people (or their victims) is disdain.

No Empathy

Psychopaths tend to be generally cold-hearted and unable to connect emotionally to other people. They don't feel concern or empathy regarding the damages they may have inflicted on other people, and they never feel a sense of loss. Psychopaths are often inconsiderate of other people's needs, and can be ruthless and tactless.

The Inability To Feel

A psychopath technically isn't a robot devoid of emotions, but he's close to one. He doesn't feel things the way "normal" people do. Although he might appear gregarious and even affectionate, his range of feelings and emotions is limited to the point of being nonexistent.

Poor Control Over Their Temper

Psychopaths often have anger management issues and violent tendencies precisely because they cannot control their behavior and expressions. They easily show signs of annoyance, anger, irritation, and impatience with other people, sometimes even with explosive and dangerous bouts of threatening and verbal and physical abuse.

Predatory Behavior

Psychopaths feed on other people. Because they often have unstable lives and careers, they intentionally find someone to manipulate to do their bidding. Instead of working to support themselves, they choose to use someone else to ensure their financial security. They can't hold regular jobs because they are looking for something grander (and more exciting) for themselves.

Impulsiveness

Psychopaths are very easy to distract, which is why they never hold on to long-term goals in life. Once they are gripped with an idea, a frustration or desire to do something, they throw all caution to the wind and proceed spontaneously to get what they want.

Never Taking Responsibility For Their Actions

When things go wrong in their plans, psychopaths never take the blame. It's always someone else's fault, and they make sure everybody knows it.

View Life In A Fantastical Way

Psychopaths always feel that they are "special" and that there are great things in store for them. They may suffer grandiose delusions about their self-worth, that they are kings or queens on their own private universe. They feel that they deserve only the best of everything—they won't settle for anything less, and they will do everything in their power to get what they want.

Always Seeking Gratification

There's nothing that matters more to a psychopath than personal gains and gratification, be it a desire for revenge against people who crossed him or a desire for monetary gain from his exploits.

Chapter Six: Different Signs and Symptoms of Mental Illness

The most common signs and symptoms of an impending or present mental illness are depression, anxiety, paranoia, insecurity, and withdrawal from society. These are also the sub-factors that contribute to the development of mental illness in a person. These symptoms or sub-factors are normally found in meek people or people with low self esteem, but this does not imply that they suffer from a mental illness. To be considered mentally ill, a person's symptoms must be of above normal levels, meaning extreme.

Depression

Depression is a mood in which a person feels down due to a certain thought or situation. Prolonged depression or general depression is one of the common signs and symptoms of mental illness. Most mentally ill individuals are regularly depressed or experience loneliness and low self esteem. This contributes to the development of negative thoughts that can become involuntary overtime.

Anxiety

People can be anxious about any one thing with good reason. People who are mentally ill are anxious and have fears without valid reason, and if there are reasons, they are usually irrational or exaggerated. They react to the feared object or situation with such vigor that it 's possible they might hurt others or get hurt themselves.

Their surroundings, and people in their surroundings, are often disregarded, and the only thing that matters is the need to escape from their source of fear. In the case of anxiety, mentally ill people are so anxious that they may experience insomnia due to constant worrying.

Constant Paranoia

While paranoia is a disorder in itself, and it can be a sign or symptom of a more serious type of mental illness. Paranoia has no rational explanation for its fears, as with severe anxiety. Afflicted individuals will go to any means to avoid the feared object, or they will experience panic attacks when faced with it.

Withdrawal From The Outside World

In most cultures, loners and anti-social

individuals are not considered abnormal, only unusual. Withdrawal from society as a symptom of mental illness is usually an intense version of average lonesomeness. Avoidant people who have difficulty forming or keeping relationships and are downright antisocial are most prone to developing personality disorders. Most personality disorders share social incapability symptoms. The lack of social interaction gives more space for solace, which , while beneficial for self reflection, is not good in combination with depression and anxiety.

Without moral support or social connections, people experiencing depression and severe anxiety will have no one to help ease their inner suffering. Solace provides space for negative thinking , which enhances the overall mood of the individual, deepening depression and heightening anxiety.

How To Overcome These Symptoms

The best way to overcome mental illness, whether minor or severe, is to have moral support throughout the duration of therapy or medication. Since most conditions stem from negative and traumatic childhood experiences , there is a need for positive replacement. A person whose memory and thinking is scarred by negligence, abuse, or maltreatment will most likely develop undesirable characteristics that can alter his or her personality. Since life experiences and people are unpredictable, at some point, an occurrence could trigger the development of a mental disorder.

Chapter Seven: How To Best Deal With Mental Illness

Dealing with mental illness is not a mathematical problem to solve in the sense that there is no given formula to put in order to get the answer. Even the solution may be more than one; each different from the other.

Step One: Spot The Disorder First

The most common problem of most people affected by a mental illness is that they don't know they have been undergoing the trauma yet. Acknowledging the problem is half the problem solved. Knowing that you have a disorder is the first step to any treatment. As long as you stay in the dark about your problem you are not going to even start recovering. Look out for signs and symptoms of common mental disorders.

Step Two: Single Out The Root Of The Problem

There is always one cause of any mental disorder. Some accident or unfortunate event like someone passing away or getting fired from the workplace might be the reason you are down in the ditch. After having singled out the root cause, it's easier to work on it because now you know what exactly is it that needs to be tackled. This stage helps you narrow down the wide variety of problems that might be plaguing you.

Step Three: Differentiate Between The Symptoms and The Cause

It is very important that you do not get confused between symptoms and cause. Signs like locking yourself inside your room, getting addicted to smoking and getting into depression are not causes; they are mere symptoms. Causes could range from breaking up with your romantic interest to losing someone very dear to you. Most people confuse themselves while trying to figure out what's the symptom and what's the cause.

Step Four: Ask A Professional For Help

If you are not mentally equipped to take on the disorder all by yourself, seeking a psychiatrist's help could be a great help. Some problems are not meant to be handled alone. An expert in the field of psychology might just help you recover in the right direction. It is advisable to seek such help from the very start so you don't end up spending time and effort in the wrong direction.

Look up online about the local psychologists in your area or ask around your social circles about one. Make sure to not spill all the beans about your disorders while doing so. Some people are judgmental about mental disorders; so it might be in your best interest to not many people know about it.

Step Five: Be Social

Sometimes all that needs to be done is mingle. Many mental disorders have been known to have been cured by a simple prescription suggesting socialization. That of course doesn't imply you should host parties and invite all the neighbors. You can always call up a close friend and go on an outing. Or get involved in workplace hang outs that are common in all offices.

Opening up to the society isn't always bad and doesn't make you an extrovert; just like staying indoors doesn't make you an introvert. Spending time with others is as important spending time with you.

Step Six: Think Positively

Quit all negative thoughts and start inviting positive ones. Those who start their mornings with a nice thought in mind have been found to have lived longer than others who didn't, according to a recent research done on human approaches. The way you think decides not only your mood for the day but also others'.

Approaching an issue with an optimistic way can always have an edge over doing the same with a negative one. It also puts your image in a good light in front of others. You get noticed in your workplace and social circles. Your ability to handle things however tricky they may be, is interpreted as a talent of yours. Before you know it, it might lead to you getting promoted or being trusted with important projects in the office.

Step Seven: Become A Quitter

Now, I am not telling you to quit everything that you are currently doing. What I mean is that if you are addicted to drugs or alcohol, put your foot down and yell, " I quit.", and stick to it. Ignoring your addiction will only lead it to escalate and before you could blink, it'd have reached heights, often beyond your control. Identify your addiction and try making attempts to quit it. It's easier said than done but once you start trying, the results are bound to come out. Trying and failing is better than not trying at all.

Step Eight: Be Wary of Medication

It is a gross myth that medication holds the ultimate cures to all the diseases in the world. In cases of mental disorders, it's the patient's determination and will power that eventually do the trick and not any number of pills. Medicines are designed to help you through the process of recovery.

Leaving the world to them and expecting to get well simply on medicines is the foulest crime one can do to one's body. Doctors can prescribe only what will assist you in the treatment. Even most mental disorder medicines only kill the symptoms and not the root cause. It is your job to work upon the latter.

Step Nine: Use Rehab As A Last Resort

Rehab centers are places where all the rejected and helpless people try to find a cure. It should be kept in mind that rehab therapy should be kept lowest in the priority list. Rehab therapy works on the principle of isolation. This isolation is immediate and strict. You will be made to suffer through withdrawal symptoms and mental agony.

While the method doe work at times, but most patients tumble further down in rehabs. It therefore becomes a loop of sorts. Most rehab institutions are poorly maintained and hardly supervised. There are people with all imaginable mental conditions present in the centre. It becomes not only uncomfortable but also risky to be among such people.

Step Ten: Do Not Look For Sympathy

It is seen as a common trend among mentally suffering patients that they tend to gain sympathy by over portraying themselves as people who are mentally touched. This practice is not just wrong but also unfair. Many criminals come up with defenses of mental incompetence to escape trials. It is a queer fashion these days to be considered special because of being afflicted with a mental disorder.

Movies have been showing protagonists as having a different mental level which if often considered eccentric by the society but secretly he is special and does heroic deeds. Such projections of mental disorders are misleading and unhelpful. Using the mental card to gain compassion or come across as special is degrading for your mentality.

Step Eleven: Try To Keep Your Emotions In Check

Emotions are the most volatile elements of the mind; more so when you are suffering from a disorder of the mind. If emotions are let free, they may get converted to harmful actions. Although those people who are suffering from mental disorders are advised to vent out, make sure you are venting out to the right person and at the right time.

Do not pick someone who's not close or is disinterested in you. Go for a dear friend or one of your siblings who would listen. Make sure the leash you put is not too tight either. Bottling up your sentiments often leads to random outbursts that have drastic effects on you and others around you. Do let out your steam; but in parts and in the right circumstances.

Step Twelve: Don't Not Ignore Help

No one has recovered from self introspection and meditation alone. Medicinal help is also necessary to put you back on track after a nasty bout of depression.

Step Thirteen: Give Medication A Try

Your body consists of certain 'pressure points', and these points require re awakening once in a while. It is widely believed that performing certain exercise of Yoga can help you do the same. These points are otherwise known as chakras.

The more you focus your mind on one point, the better these chakras function. They regulate the energy flow and distribution throughout our bodies. There are believed to be seven of them, placed all along our spine, working tirelessly to keep us running. Chakras determine the entire functioning of your system. Keep them healthy and your mind will automatically follow suit.

Step Fourteen: Develop A Bond With Your Psychiatrist

In what has become to be known as the newest trend in the psychological field, patients are encouraged to develop personal relationships with their psychiatrist. These help in in-session analysis of the patients and help the psychiatrist grasp a better idea of what the patient is going through. This method is medically known as functional analytical psychotherapy. The fundamental difference between this and ordinary psychotherapy is that things are more personal and hence clearer in the former while the former is merely based on generally drawn assumptions and theoretically mugged routines.

Step Fifteen: Guard Against A Never-Ending Cycle

What is more dangerous than the mental disorder that's affecting you is it turning into a cycle on its own. For example, you have an OCD (Obsessive Compulsive disorder) that makes you to arrange your books in alphabetical order to be placed on your shelf. When you give in to it, you are completing the cycle and making way for another. Do not let cycles get completed by resisting from succumbing to the temptation. It may take tremendous will power to do so but once you have started forming a habit, it'll get easier with each next time it returns.

Some Other Helpful Tips

Even if you don't feel like it, make the effort to set aside time do something that is both enjoyable and therapeutic such as taking up yoga, meditation, or planting a garden.

1. Take care of your body by avoiding alcohol and tobacco, eating nutritious meals, and getting enough sleep.

2. Practice coping skills. There are many on-the-spot stress strategies that last just a minute or so, one of them being learning how to breathe properly.

3. Surround yourself with contented people; people who are positive, happy, and who can support you.

4. It can help to look away from your own problems and make a concerted effort to help someone else, whether it is a child, an old person, someone in hospital, or a lonely pet in a shelter.

5. Animals themselves are very therapeutic and will never condemn you.

Get The Help When You Need It

Contrary to what some people think, being willing to get help is a wonderful, positive sign of strength, and if you get help early you will find that you are able to recover from your mental illness and lead a fulfilling life. There are many services and organizations that offer help and support if you suspect you have a mental health problem, or that you could develop one. Remember that most people can recover without the need to go into hospital and this applies to you too.

There are specialist services that provide a 24-hour counseling service. Different health professionals offer different kinds of services and treatments, which are directed at the particular mental problem you have. The people who can help you will be social workers, psychiatrists, psychologists, complementary health practitioners, or general practitioners.

Some hospitals have day programs and there are also outpatient programs, which are conducted by trained mental health workers. Psychosocial treatments provide support and guidance, and they will include help for your family members too. Some of these treatments include:

1. Cognitive Behavioral Therapy

This is a talking therapy where you are taught how to manage your problems by actually changing the way you think. It isn't a treatment that takes away mental illness, but rather works at helping you deal with your problems in a more positive way.

2. Psycho Education

Education will be offered to you as someone with a mental health condition as well as your family. The education is designed to empower you so that you can deal with your condition.

The idea behind psycho-education is that with a clear understanding of the mental condition you have or may be developing, you will be equipped to deal with the problem and contribute to your own emotional well being.

3. Psychotherapy

This treatment is based on the relationship between the psychologist and you. The idea is to be able to talk openly in a safe and supportive environment to someone who is neutral and nonjudgmental. The therapist will work with you to change your thoughts and behavior. The therapist will also teach you new skills to cope with situations that would otherwise set you back.

4. Supplmentation

With omega 3, folate, and vitamin B has been found to be very useful in the management of mental illness, and you may want to include these supplements in your diet.

If you have been diagnosed with a mental illness or you suspect you may be on the way to developing a mental disorder , there is relief from the symptoms of your mental illness because there are so many specialized treatment plans available for each of the many mental illnesses.

If you have Internet access, you will discover that there are even e-therapies available. There is a direct link between a healthy mind and the immune system, and many illnesses can develop if you are constantly experiencing mental anguish. Learning techniques to relax and calm yourself will certainly help your body's ability to heal itself. You will find that you become less restless, you regain some form of control, and you will be able to face life's challenges with a fighting attitude.

Chapter Eight: Real Life Solutions To Conquer Your Mental Illness In Your Personal Life and In Society

This chapter contains a comprehensive account of how participants succeeded to resolve life is a struggle. It presents their long and arduous journey that led them to devise real-life solutions to manage their own personal lives successfully. This chapter includes details from real participants and how they managed to conquer their mental illness using powerful strategies.

Stage 1: Dealing With Life Is A Constant Struggle

Entry into the first stage of transforming oneself occurred with the advent of the struggle with having a mental disorder. Two phases were identified: not wanting to deal with anything and trying to get on top of having a mental disorder.

Phase One: Not Wanting To Deal With Anything

Participants frankly stated that in this first phase they did not want to deal with anything in life: "Not have to deal with anything". They said that this phase most often occurred at the beginning of an episode, especially in the first few years of an illness, and when stress became too much to handle.

In their powerlessness due to the cumulative nature of aspects of life is a struggle, participants turned to the only strategy they could think of and employ at this point of not wanting to deal with anything, that is, to withdraw.

Phase Two: Trying To Conquer The Mental illness On Your Own

In this second phase of trying to deal with life is a struggle participants were looking at all possibilities as to what to do "to try and get on top of their mental disorder. After their failure at not wanting to deal with anything participants' focus now changed to trying to get on top of having a mental disorder. They said that they wanted nothing more than to get rid of it and, in addition, society placed great emphasis on it: "The focus on the mental illness was huge."

The main goal of this phase was to become 100% normal, which is no easy feat. Participants said that being normal would give them the chance to organize themselves, have sufficient mental energy and would not be miserable anymore , all without having to resort to taking medications.

Stage Two: The Turning Point

The separation between stage 1 and stage 2 of transforming oneself was the turning point. A turning point is defined as "a point at which decisive changes take place; a critical point." Participants turned from being powerless at trying to deal with life is a struggle despite their best efforts, to discovering ways to gain power over what to do.

Multiple studies have found that a turning point was necessary in order to achieve the transformation that ultimately turned participants' life is a struggle into a life of being at peace. The turning point was either precipitated by a crisis or brought on by empowering experiences whether that be a crisis or finding the power within oneself.

Stage Three: Getting Better As A Person

Participants started on a new trajectory by taking the most important lesson learnt in stage 1 to heart, namely that they could not get on top of having a mental disorder. They now realized that they had to take a much broader view by going "far beyond the boundaries of mental illness and the biomedical model ."

They had to change their focus onto what was pivotal to life is a struggle, that is , the struggle to identify any intrinsic value in oneself as a person , and resolve that first.

Getting better as a person had a personal and a social dimension. The following participant illustrated the personal dimension: "I want to get stronger. I want to be able to cope better". The social dimension pertained to participants' getting better as a person in their relationship with other people: "The only thing that makes a person better or worse is this: you are better if you can do good things like helping other people and you are worse if you do bad things like hurting other people."

Step One: Developing A New and Positive Identity For Yourself

Through refocusing away from trying to get on top of having a mental disorder onto getting better as a person participants grasped the opportunity to look anew at who they were as a person. It slowly dawned on them that they had attributes that did not belong to the disempowered picture drawn up by society, and which they had so completely adopted in the pivotal struggle to identify any intrinsic value in oneself as a person.

They realized that these attributes, hitherto obscured, indeed belonged to them and could be used to lay the foundation to build a new identity that was positive. That was the start for their enduring empowerment.

Participants in numerous studies discovered three significant attributes in themselves that became part of their new, positive identity: the ability to make choices, self-reliance and determination.

Step Two: Learning New Strategies

After having gained a new, positive identity, and before taking action, getting better as a person could now progress to devising new strategies. Participants thought of four new strategies: formulating new goals, having a plan ready, using constructive ways of dealing with problems, and developing new skills.

The first new strategy started with "wiping my slate clean." Participants reasoned that any old goals from stage 1 had to be got rid of and new goals set so that the new strategies could reflect them.

The second new strategy was to have a plan of what to do ready for when another episode loomed. Participants stated that being proactive in this way reduced the helplessness experienced as part of the struggle with having a mental disorder. Having a plan ready consisted of increasing medications oneself straightaway before accessing medical help.

The third new strategy in this study was to use constructive rather than destructive ways of dealing with problems. Using constructive ways prevented the disastrous consequences of using extreme measures that had damaged both participants and their relationship with other people in trying to get on top of having a mental disorder.

Stage Four: Finally Being At Peace

The conclusion to transforming oneself, encapsulated as being at peace, signaled to participants that the long and arduous journey towards resolving life is a struggle was complete: There is no doubt about it, it has been a struggle to have got to that resolution and peace. Participants described being at peace as being at peace with the fact that they had a mental disorder, with their place in society, and with who they were as a person.

<u>Conclusion</u>

If you are someone caught in the quagmire of mental disorder, notice the signs and their frequencies. Do not panic. Contact the nearest psychiatrist and set up a date. Start attending the sessions as soon as possible. Stick to the prescription and religiously take your pills. If you think that was enough, you and I are using different dictionaries to define 'enough'.

Replace your current approach with a healthier one. Computers are shut down; not humans. Open up about your issue by talking to someone you hold close. Meditate to keep your mind free of distractions. It is not sufficient that you ensure normalcy only internally. Your mind's health is directly proportional to your body's fitness.

Your body and mind are two conveniently connected and mutually functional entities.

One gets shot down; the other gets weakened. Similarly, one gets a boost; the other starts gaining from it! To ensure that your mind is recovering well from your recent mental disorder, take good care of your body. Exercise well and eat good. Include all the nutrition you can in your diet and join a gym if your Body Mass Index is inappropriate.

It's often from others that we look for inspiration. And who better to draw motivation from than the great personalities of the globe? Another thing you can do ward off whatever fragments of the mental illness must be left in you is to keep yourself busy in anything that pleases your tastes. It could be a hobby or a habit. Reading, gardening, sewing, or writing. These are more of engagements than distractions.

Hopefully, this book has succeeded in its goal of broadening your understanding of personality disorders and mental illnesses , and may it also aid you in coping with the the tendencies that surround yourself and your loved ones.

One thing to remember about mental illness is that diagnoses of most conditions are based on what is normal or accepted in a culture. While severe anxiety is considered a mental condition in some countries, it is disregarded in others. In undeveloped places, mental disorders are perceived as possessions, curses, or results of witchcraft. However, only professionals can diagnose mental illnesses.

Remember, if there's one person stopping you from achieving what you want; it's you. Let yourself heal. We all make memories and sometimes they turn out to be bad ones. It doesn't mean life stops; it may halt but stop? That's preposterous to the point of idiocy. So take control and own up if you find something wrong. Like we said earlier – only you can help yourself.

About Us

The Thought Flame is committed to add value to its customers through various books, online courses and other resources. You can learn more about us and our books at www.thethoughtflame.com.

Don't forget to check out our amazing **online video courses** at www.thethoughtflame.com/courses/ to take your knowledge to another level.

To check out our **extraordinary collection of diet/cookbooks**, visit http://www.thethoughtflame.com/category/non-fictional/cookbooks/ .

As a part of our valued relationship with our customers, we keep providing you free promotional books, courses and other stuff on subscribing with us on our site. We have a strict anti-spam policy and assure you no spam mails will be sent to your mailbox.

To subscribe with us, visit

www.thethoughtflame.com.

Like our work and would like to say thanks?

Buy us a cup of coffee at

www.thethoughtflame.com/coffee/

Author

Amarpreet Singh is an avid learner and his passion for education has made him travel, work and study all across the world. He holds three masters degrees, including MBA, from top universities in Asia.

He is author of dozens of books, many of which are Amazon's bestseller, varying in various topics and categories. He also teaches many online courses having thousands of students across the world.

He has a keen interest in international affairs, economics, global poverty and politics, financial markets and entrepreneurship, and strives to be part of a community that shares the same passion.

He has worked as consultant with organizations like Airbus and The World Bank.

He loves travelling and learning about new cultures, and has been fortunate to live/work/travel/study in countries like India, China, Korea, US, South Africa, Japan, Philippines, Singapore, Canada etc., and learn about the culture and lifestyle in each of them.

To check out more of his work, visit www.thethoughtflame.com

www.ingramcontent.com/pod-product-compliance
Lightning Source LLC
Chambersburg PA
CBHW020901310526
45786CB00018B/1351